Creativity in Communities

T0017045

Heather Gallagher

Reader Consultants

Cheryl Norman Lane, M.A.Ed.
Classroom Teacher
Chino Valley Unified School District

Jennifer M. Lopez, M.S.Ed., NBCT
Teacher Specialist—History/Social Studies
Norfolk Public Schools

iCivics Consultants

Emma Humphries, Ph.D.
Chief Education Officer

Taylor Davis, M.T.
Director of Curriculum and Content

Natacha Scott, MAT
Director of Educator Engagement

Publishing Credits

Rachelle Cracchiolo, M.S.Ed., *Publisher*
Emily R. Smith, M.A.Ed., *VP of Content Development*
Véronique Bos, *Creative Director*
Dona Herweck Rice, *Senior Content Manager*
Dani Neiley, *Associate Content Specialist*
Fabiola Sepulveda, *Series Designer*

Image Credits: p.5 Natalia Babok/iStock /pp.6–9 (composites) Fabiola Sepulveda;
pp.10–11 Judy Griesedieck; pp.12–13 Illegal Art (www.illegalart.org); p.14 Tanya Hart via
Flickr; p.15 Andrew Harker/Shutterstock; pp.16–17 Chicago Botanic Garden; p.18 (right)
Bart Everson via Flickr; p.19 courtesy Community Visions Unlimited; p.20 ATLbiker via
Wikicommons; p.21 (top) Onehiroki via Wikicommons; p.21 (bottom) Robert Neff;
p.23 (top) © WashedAshore.org; p.23 (bottom) Damon Higgins/The Palm Beach Post via ZUMA
Wire/Newscom; pp.24–25 Jonathan Alcorn/ZUMA Press/Alamy; p.25 (top) Joe Sohm Universal
Images Group/Newscom; pp.26–27 David Grossman/Alamy; p.28 Lucy Brown/iStock;
p.29 Frances M. Roberts/Newscom; all other images from iStock and/or Shutterstock

Library of Congress Cataloging-in-Publication Data

Names: Gallagher, Heather, author.
Title: Creativity in communities / Heather Gallagher.
Description: Huntington Beach, CA : Teacher Created Materials, 2020. |
  Includes index. | Audience: Grades 2-3 | Summary: "All around the
  country, people are working to make their communities better. They are
  gardening, painting, singing, and more. And they are doing it all
  together! Learn more about how people find ways to be creative in their
  communities"-- Provided by publisher.
Identifiers: LCCN 2020016265 (print) | LCCN 2020016266 (ebook) | ISBN
  9781087605098 (paperback) | ISBN 9781087619286 (ebook)
Subjects: LCSH: Community arts projects--United States--Juvenile
  literature. | Artists and community--United States--Juvenile literature.
Classification: LCC NX180.A77 G35 2020 (print) | LCC NX180.A77 (ebook) |
  DDC 700.1/030973--dc23
LC record available at https://lccn.loc.gov/2020016265
LC ebook record available at https://lccn.loc.gov/2020016266

This book may not be reproduced or distributed in any
way without prior written consent from the publisher.

5482 Argosy Avenue
Huntington Beach, CA 92649-1039
www.tcmpub.com

ISBN 978-1-0876-0509-8

© 2022 Teacher Created Materials, Inc.

The name "iCivics" and the iCivics logo are
registered trademarks of iCivics, Inc.
Printed in China
WaiMan

Table of Contents

Creative Communities

How do you feel when you create? Art is a great way of showing how you feel. You can use art to say you are happy. You can use art to say you are sad. You can use art to connect with other people. And you can even use art to spark awareness and change in your community!

These artists draw with chalk on the street.

This artist paints in her workshop.

All over the nation, people are coming together to make art. They make art in schools, in town halls, and on streets. At the same time, they make friends. They improve their communities too. Many of these projects do not require special talent. They are fun activities that anyone can do. You can do them too!

Jump into Fiction

Flat Alex on an Adventure

Hi, I'm Alex. I've just gotten back from a trip with my aunt. Aunt Martha is an artist. We took a trip to see the projects she's working on. It was a success! Well...mostly a success. Wait, I'm getting ahead of myself.

My story begins when I first got to Aunt Martha's house. I thought I would draw a Flat Alex. Do you know the book *Flat Stanley* by Jeff Brown? It's about a kid who gets flattened by a noticeboard. Even though Flat Stanley is, well, flat, he has all sorts of adventures. I wanted Flat Alex to have adventures too! And, wow, we sure did! We went to beaches and mountains. We saw cities and farms. There was so much to see and do. Then, Aunt Martha added a fun, new twist!

One day, Aunt Martha said she had a surprise. It was an art project called "Letters to Me." For the project, we would write letters to our future selves. We would also draw pictures on the letters of things we saw and did. Then, we would ask someone to mail us our letters in about six months. It was such a cool idea!

I spent a lot of time thinking about what I wanted to write and draw. I wanted to remember how special the trip had been. For example, I wrote about how Flat Alex and I helped paint a GIANT mural. And I wrote about the big sand castle we made after seeing a fancy sand castle contest. Then, I sealed the envelope and handed it in.

When we went to leave, I realized my mistake. I had put Flat Alex in the envelope! Sorry, Flat Alex...I guess I'll see you in six months!

Back to Nonfiction

The Northeast

Ellen Griesedieck loves making big art. And her American **Mural** Project is BIG! The mural shows people working. She says the mural inspires kids to think about what they want to be when they grow up.

The mural is made from all sorts of materials. Some parts are painted. Some parts are made with glass. There is even a part made from old watches! More than 15,000 people from around the world have added to it so far! It is like a giant puzzle. Griesedieck sets aside a special spot for each piece while it is made.

Griesedieck helps students design their part of the mural.

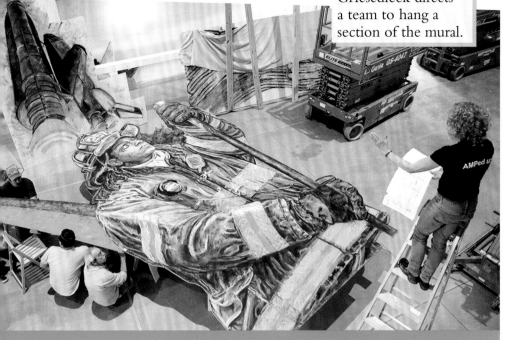

Griesedieck directs a team to hang a section of the mural.

Each year, the mural grows bigger. It hangs in a former **mill** in Connecticut. The mill's roof had to be raised to fit the mural! People can see and study the mural as it grows. They can see what happens when people come together through art.

A Truly American Mural

Griesedieck can't finish her project on her own. Luckily, lots of people want to help! Her goal is to have at least one person from each state add to the mural.

The Illegal Art program is another community art example. It started with some New York artists and their common goals. They wanted to make the world a better place while also helping people feel like part of something big. So they came up with projects that would be easy to join. Each project is meant for people to complete and share. Sometimes, the artists paint big questions that they want people to answer. Sometimes, the artists post "I Spy" signs for people to write on.

The Illegal Art artists find fun ways to get people involved. One example is their "To Me" project. The plan was to capture a moment in time for each person. First, people choose from a wall of blank postcards. Then, they write a note to their "future self" and give the card back. In six months, the notes are mailed to them. The goal of the project is to honor people's past and future selves.

Think and Talk

What would you write in a note to your future self?

The Midwest

In 2019, a group in Corning, Iowa, wanted to honor soldiers who had died. It had been 100 years since **World War I** ended. More than 3,000 soldiers from Iowa died in the war. So, the group came up with a plan. They would **knit** and **crochet** (crow-SHAY) poppies. Poppies are a type of flower. They are also a symbol for people who have died in wars. The Iowa poppies, though, would be made of fabric. Flowers can die quickly. Poppies made of yarn will last longer.

This woman made a string of knitted poppies.

The group in Iowa wanted a lot of poppies. So they asked for help. They were amazed by the response! People sent in thousands of poppies. With that many poppies, each soldier could be honored.

The group placed the poppies in a park. They made a colorful display. The poppies also became part of a special art show. The show is called These Fallen Friends.

Crochet Connections

The Crochet Guild of America has thousands of members. The goal of this group is to help people connect through crocheting. The group also helps new people learn how to crochet.

These knitted poppies are part of a World War I memorial.

LEST WE FORGET

Art is not the only way for a community to be creative. In 2003, the Windy City **Harvest** Youth Farm program began. The Youth Farm program is based in Chicago, Illinois. Around 90 teenagers work for Youth Farm each year. The program teaches them how to farm and cook healthy food. It also teaches them how to sell their **produce** at local markets.

The Youth Farm program has grown a lot since it started. During its first year, there was just one farm. Now, there are more than 10 farms. They are spread in and near Chicago. Some of the farms are even on rooftops! The Youth Farm workers there get a great view of the city while they work.

A Youth Farm worker takes care of a crop.

Food Deserts

The Youth Farm sells most of its crops to "food deserts." These are places that do not have easy access to healthy foods. The Youth Farm has grown and sold over 100,000 pounds (45 metric tons) of produce to food deserts! That is the same weight as 30 cars!

Youth Farm workers take pride in their work.

The South

In 1993, a group in New Orleans, Louisiana, formed Community Visions Unlimited (CVU). Their goal was to find a way to add art to their city. So, they hired local artists to paint **utility boxes**. The plain gray boxes were changed into works of art.

At first, artists painted in just one neighborhood. Then, Hurricane Katrina hit New Orleans in 2005. CVU wanted to help. So, they expanded the program to nearby areas. Local artists have now painted more than 230 utility boxes! They decorate the cities and have a lot of community support.

blank utility box

A CVU artist works on her box design.

Each neighborhood describes what they want their boxes to look like. Then, CVU picks a local artist to design and paint the box. CVU gives the artists paint and supplies. The artists also get recognition for their work.

Think and Talk

How do the photos on these pages help explain what the author is talking about?

In 1999, a student in Atlanta, Georgia, thought of a way to improve the city. Ryan Gravel saw miles of old, unused railway tracks. He thought those tracks could be changed into something new. He wrote to local leaders about his plans. They thought his idea was great!

The transformed area is called the Atlanta BeltLine. The BeltLine offers fun things for people to do. They can enjoy the parks and green spaces. They can visit the new skate park. They can also enjoy the miles of art that are there.

Art has been part of the BeltLine since 2010. Each year, artists display new works of art. All the art is free to view. There are murals and **sculptures**. There are photographs and performances. There are even days where non-artists can go to the BeltLine and paint alongside some of Atlanta's most famous artists!

This BeltLine art is under a bridge.

Plenty to See

There are more than 450 performances and works of art for guests to see at the Atlanta BeltLine. That is not all! There are bike trails and hiking trails. There are farms and fitness classes. The Atlanta BeltLine has something for everyone!

These sculptures look like they are walking along a BeltLine trail.

The West

In Portland, Oregon, the Washed Ashore Project is making art with a message. Angela Haseltine Pozzi founded the project. She was shocked at how much plastic washes up on local beaches. She wanted to bring attention to the **pollution** problem. So, Pozzi made ocean-themed art out of the plastic she found.

The Washed Ashore Project has grown quickly. More than 10,000 volunteers have helped clean beaches. Artists have turned these plastic pieces into more than 70 sculptures.

The Washed Ashore Project takes these sculptures on tour. Pozzi wants people to see the problem firsthand. And she does not plan on stopping anytime soon. Pozzi says that she will keep working until "we run out of plastic on the beach."

Pollution harms ocean animals.

Work begins on a
Washed Ashore fish.

Priscilla the Parrot Fish
is made of plastic.

Venice, California, is known for its art and culture. The Venice Art Walls are located at the heart of Venice Beach. They are famous around the world. Part of what makes the Art Walls unique is that it is legal to **graffiti** there. In most places, graffiti is illegal. At the Art Walls, it is encouraged! People can bring cans of spray paint and show off their skills.

Another part of what makes the Art Walls unique is that all people are welcome to add to it. You do not have to be a professional artist. Thousands of people from around the world have made their mark there. Because of this, one section of wall has more than 8,000 pounds (3.6 metric tons) of paint!

Paint Permission

The Art Walls are one of the only places in the country where graffiti is legal. The only limit is that artists must apply for a **permit** first. The permits tell artists where to paint so that they don't cover up someone else's work. Permits are free, so anyone can get one!

Good for You

Doctors have found that making art is a way to stay healthy! Making art can help people feel less stressed. It can help people relax. Making art can even help people remember better.

Across America

There are interesting projects taking place all over the country. Art and other creative projects can be ways to express how you feel. They can help you speak your mind. They can be ways to connect with other people. You can use the projects to make people happy. You can use them to bring people together. You can use them to make old spaces look new again.

Taking part in these projects can help people feel good. Doctors know that people feel better when they think creatively. Doctors know that looking at art can make people feel better too. When art and other creative projects involve an entire community, the impact is even greater!

Everyone can make their mark on their community. The first step is to find projects nearby. Or you can go to a local art show or community center. You can see what other people are doing to improve the area around you. They can help you learn more. They can help you think of new ideas too.

Maybe one day you will start your own community project. You can start small. Small projects can have big impacts! You will improve your community and find personal benefits at the same time. You will get to know people better. You may find new ways to help others. You may find a way to make someone's day a bit brighter. And, you will also learn a lot and have fun!

People make art with dyed sawdust.

Calling All Craftivists!

One art style that is on the rise across the country is *craftivism*. The term craftivism joins two words—*craft* and *activism*. *Activism* is the use of actions to cause things to change. Craftivists use arts and crafts to make change.

Glossary

crochet—perform a type of needlework that involves weaving loops of thread with a hooked needle

graffiti—writing or drawing on a public surface

harvest—to gather a crop

knit—perform a type of needlework that involves crossing pieces of yarn with needles

mill—building where people use machines to grind grain into flour

mural—a work of art where paint or other materials are added to a wall

permit—a written statement that says someone can do something

pollution—substances that make water, land, or air dirty and not suitable or safe for use

produce—fresh fruits and vegetables

sculptures—artwork that is made by carving hard substances, molding plastics, or melting metals

utility boxes—metal boxes that contain electrical equipment

World War I—a war that was fought mainly in Europe between 1914 and 1918

Index

Civics in Action

Volunteers help make their communities better. But these things do not just happen. Someone must lead them. Sometimes, they need a group name. This way, people know what they are all about. You can create an activity for a volunteer group to help your community.

1. Decide on an activity to help your community. Be creative!

2. Name your volunteer group.

3. Explain how people can volunteer.

4. Make a plan. Tell where and when you need people to work. Tell them what they will be doing.

5. Design a webpage or poster where people can learn about your group and how they can help.